# Reaching Out To The Hurting World With The Love of God

## Thelma Nkomo

**Produced for BTN Books**
## WORD2PRINT
A Division of One-Touch UK

**Reaching Out to the Hurting World
With the Love of God**

Copyright © 2013 Thelma Nkomo

Bishop Thelma Nkomo can be reached via email:
bishopthelmankomo@yahoo.co.uk
Unless otherwise stated, all Scripture quotations are taken
from New King James Version (NKJV) of the Bible. Scriptures
taken from Holy Bible, New International Version®, NIV®
Copyright © 1973, 1978, 1984, 2011 by Biblica, Inc.® Used
by permission. All rights reserved worldwide.

First published in the United Kingdom in 2013 by BTN Books
ISBN 978-0-957609-80-8
Produced for BTN Books by Word2Print
www.word2print.com

A CIP catalogue record for this title is available from the
British Library

*Printed and bound by
CPI Group (UK) Ltd, Croydon, CR0 4YY*

# Contents

## *Dedication*

*I would like to dedicate this book to my children Langa,
Bekezela and Ruth.
Through it all we have learnt to trust in Jesus.
Thank you for your constant love, support, and
appreciation.*

*I love you all.*

# Introduction

Millions of people across the nations of the earth have been hurt by one person, or another. They have been hurt by people they love so dearly - friends, family, fellow church members, pastors, and work colleagues. Many, I daresay, have been hurt by losing loved ones through uncontrollable events like war. It may be that you are one of those who are hurt, or even the one hurting others. This book has the answers for you; so I urge you to take your time to read it.

The world is hurting, because there is no love without hypocrisy (Romans 12: 9a). There are two commandments, which are considered to be the greatest. The first is: "You shall love the Lord thy God with all your heart, with all your soul, and with all your mind". (Matthew 22:37). The second is like it: "You shall love your neighbour as yourself" (Matthew 22:39a). On these two commandments hang all the Law and the Prophets. (Matthew 22:40).

I pray that after reading this book, there will be

a change of heart towards those who have hurt you. And for those who have hurt others, my prayer is they will have repentant hearts. May the God of love, revelation, peace, knowledge, and understanding be with you as you go through the pages of this book. May you be filled with the love of God, so you may be able to extend the love that God has so freely given to us.

Together, let us change the world with the Love of God. Let love be without hypocrisy. Abhor what is evil. Cling to what is good. Be kindly affectionate to one another with brotherly love, in honour giving preference to one another (Romans 12:9-10).

*Thelma Nkomo*
*London, June 2013*

# Acknowledgements

First I would like to thank God Almighty for saving my soul and for giving me wisdom knowledge and understanding. I thank Him for taking me out of darkness into light to know His love that passes all knowledge so that I can share His love throughout the world.

I would like to express my gratitude to all the people who have contributed to the writing of this book. I would like to thank you for your encouragement and your support all the way. May the Lord richly bless you as His message of love spreads across the world.

*Thelma Nkomo*
*London, June 2013*

The world is hurting…

Only the love of God can bring healing.

# 1

# Love: The Key to Creation

**G**OD has sent me to reach out to the hurting world with His love. God says the world is hurting because there is no love from a pure heart. His admonition to us is to 'love without hypocrisy' (Romans 12:9-10). In my spiritual walk and through my ministry, I have come across so many people who have been really hurt in their lives. Some of the things I have heard are so deep and painful that it would take only the grace and the love of God for them to overcome.

When God first sent me out to reach out to the hurting world with His love, I did not realise how badly people were hurting, even in the Body of Christ. Most people have never shared their pain with anyone due to the fear of reprisal, especially in the matters of sexual abuse, which may have happened in their early years. Most men and women who are hurting now were abused in their childhood but have never mentioned it to anyone because of fear that they will be blamed for it. Some people have told somebody, but have been even more hurt because they were not given the right reception. In other words, there was no compassion given to them; only judgement. Some have been wounded by bad words uttered to them, some have been put down, and some have been falsely accused, rejected, and discriminated against.

Some people lose their self-esteem because they have been told that they are useless, they cannot do anything, and that they are a waste of space. As they grow up being tortured by those negative words, they struggle to fit into society, and as a result some end up doing foolish things - so they can be accepted or loved. Sadly, many look for alternative love and affection in the wrong places.

As humans, we tend to see each other differently when the love of God is not in our hearts. The world also makes us to treat each other differently for selfish gains. We feel we are more superior to the other person. The world system puts us in different categories, and people then belong to the so-called upper, middle and lower classes. To make it more segregating, each of these classes is further divided into lower, middle and upper segments. You may ask: "What are these classes measured by?" Riches, material things, and occupational group that people belong to. This segregation ultimately tends to defuse the purpose of God.

This is what God said at creation:

> *Let us make man in Our image, according to Our likeness; let them have dominion over the fish of the sea, over the birds of the air, and over the cattle, over all the earth and over every creeping thing that creeps on the earth.*

Genesis 1: 26

So man was given dominion over the fish of the sea, the fowl of the air, the rest of the animals. He was also given dominion over all living and non-living things. But man was not given dominion to dominate another human being, which is where the problem with the human race lies today. We want to lord it over each other. One mortal man wants to rule, suppress, and subjugate another, irrespective of the wishes of the other person. That was not in the original plan of God at creation.

God created man in His own image; in the image of God, male and female He created them (Genesis 1:27). If we are all God's creation, why then are we divided through colour, race, language, tribe, and religion? And why are families falling apart? The answer is simply that we have no understanding about who our Creator is, why He created us, or what He requires from us. The battle starts when man's heart fails him. It all boils down to the heart. We tend to value things that have no value, instead of us valuing life that is precious. We fight for things that we did not bring to this earth, and things that we certainly will not carry with us when we leave this world

**For we brought nothing into this world, and it is certain we can carry nothing out.**

*(1 Timothy 6:7)*

My prayer today is that the Lord God Himself should help your understanding of Him and of His love.

# 2

# An Ungodly Society

**A** **SOCIETY** without God gives birth to a society full of unforgiveness, anger, malice, hatred, strife, greed, covetousness, idolatry, wickedness, pride, blasphemy, deceit, drunkenness, and witchcraft. A godless existence gives birth to a perverse generation of thieves, liars adulterers, fornicators, murderers, racists, tribalists, gangsters, paedophiles, and drug traffickers. We have excluded God from our lives today, and we are now leading an unguided life. This is why we don't understand each other, because there is no Jesus who can break the chord of tension. As stated in the previous chapter, we are programmed according to the strategies of society. We classify ourselves by social status, thereby causing divisions among people.

Segregation and divisions are not the only depravities that the act of excluding God creates in our lives. The streets are also not safe because there is no love of God. Our homes are not safe anymore because there is no love among family members. We are terrified of each other because there is no love. People do not respect one another because there is no love. Gangs are ruling the streets with knives and guns, due to the lack of love. What about gang rapes, murder, drug and human trafficking, domestic violence, greed, stealing, hatred, malice, envy, racism, tribalism and unforgiveness? They are all due to lack of understanding of God, and absence of love. Even worse, fighting and bickering happen among brethren in the Church because there is no love.

If you look at our society now, these are the things that we encounter every day. You walk on the streets looking over your shoulders. You don't feel comfortable when somebody is walking behind you. Our minds are now programmed to fear one another, and to perceive one another differently. If God created male and female in His own image, why then are we afraid of each other? Why do we hurt each other? Why do we hate one another? Why do we steal from each other? Why do we kill one another?

The Lord God, our Maker did not create us to be unequal. The devil is the one who has made us to view and treat each other differently. The serpent (which is the devil) beguiled Eve to eat fruit from the tree of knowledge of good and evil, and Eve later gave the same to Adam to eat. After Eve and Adam ate from the tree their eyes began to open and they began see themselves naked. Then, they began to notice things they did not notice about each other before. It was because they ate from the tree of the knowledge of good and evil, which God had commanded them not to eat.

Eating from that tree would have meant that Adam and Eve would die spiritually. It shows how much love God had for Adam and Eve that He protected them from doing evil and destroying themselves. When Adam and Eve ate from the tree of knowledge of good and evil, they were exposed to the evil things. The devil's seed of disobedience - to disobey God their creator - was sown into their lives by Eve, who listened to the serpent (the devil).

According to the scriptures, Adam gave birth to the nation that knew evil and good. Abel's works were righteous before God, but Cain's works were not. As a result, Cain killed his brother out of jealousy and envy (Genesis 4:1-8).

> *Now Adam knew Eve his wife, and she conceived and bore Cain and said, "I have gotten a man from the Lord." Then she bore again, this time his brother Abel. Now Abel was a keeper of sheep, but Cain was a tiller of the ground. And in process of time it came to pass, that Cain brought of the fruit of the ground to the Lord. Abel also brought of the firstborn of his flock and of their fat. And the Lord respected Abel and his offering, but He did not respect Cain and his offering. And Cain was very angry, and his countenance fell. And the Lord said to Cain, "Why are you angry? And why has your countenance fallen? If you do well, will you not be accepted? And if you do not do well, sin lies at the door. And its desire is for you, but you should rule over it. Now Cain talked with Abel his brother; and it came to pass, when they*

**were in the field, that Cain rose up against Abel his brother, and killed him.**

Genesis 4:1–8.

As we can gather from these scriptures, Cain killed his brother because he was jealous of him. Abel's works pleased God, but Cain's works did not. Abel touched God with his giving, whereas Cain's giving was not from his heart, so it displeased God. Jealousy and envy reigned in Cain's heart. From Adam's race, sin began to spread among the people, as they multiplied on the earth up to the time God destroyed the whole earth with the floods, save Noah and his children.

A lawyer once asked Jesus a crucial question: "Master, which is the greatest commandment in the law?" Jesus replied, "You shall love the Lord your God with all your heart, with all your soul, and with all your mind. This is the first and great commandment. And the second is like it: 'You shall love your neighbour as yourself. On these two commandments hang all the Law and the Prophets" (Matthew 22:35-40).

So love is the ultimate requirement.

Have you ever imagined a society walking in the love of God, with everyone greeting one another, helping each other, and caring for each other? Not only helping only those we know or love. The world would be a beautiful place to live in. Let love begin with you, as you read this book. Let us change this world together with the love of God.

# 3

# A Broken Relationship

**I**T is important to look at what became of God's relationship with man after He created man in His own image. Remember that after creation, God looked down at His creation and said everything was good (Genesis 1:31). So if everything was so good, what happened to the relationship between God and man?

In Genesis 6:1-8, God repents of creating man, as the heart of man fails him. God realises that the heart of man is evil continually, so He determines to destroy man whom He created:

> *Now it came to pass, when men began to multiply on the face of the earth, and daughters were born to them, that the sons of God saw the daughters of men, that they were beautiful; and they took wives for themselves of all whom they chose. And the Lord said "My Spirit shall not strive with man forever, for He is indeed flesh; yet his days shall be one hundred and twenty years." There were giants on the earth in those days, and also afterward, when the sons of God came in to the daughters of men and*

*they bore children to them. Those were the mighty men of old, men of renown. Then the Lord saw that the wickedness of man was great in the earth, and that every intent of the thoughts of his heart was only evil continually. And the Lord was sorry that He had made man on the earth, and He was grieved in His heart. So the Lord said, "I will destroy man whom I have created from the face of the earth, both man and beast, creeping thing and birds of the air, for I am sorry that I have made them." But Noah found grace in the eyes of the Lord.*

Now I want us to focus on Genesis 6:5 where God talks about the wickedness of man being great on the earth and that every imagination of the thoughts of his heart was only evil continually. What is 'evil' in the sight of God? Evil is everything that is not pleasing to God. Sin is sin; there is no small sin or big sin. If you are fornicating, you are the same as the murderer. In my understanding every sin that we commit starts from the heart.

Paul writes in Galatians 5:19-21

*Now the works of the flesh are evident, which are: adultery, fornication, uncleanness, lewdness, idolatry, sorcery, hatred, contentions, jealousies, outbursts of wrath, selfish ambitions, dissensions, heresies, envy, murders, drunkenness, revelries, and the like; of*

**which I tell you beforehand, just as I also told you in time past, that those who practice such things will not inherit the kingdom of God.**

Paul also writes in 1Corinthians 6:9-10

**Do you not know that the unrighteous will not inherit the kingdom of God? Do not be deceived. Neither fornicators, nor idolaters, nor adulterers, nor homosexuals, nor sodomites, nor thieves, nor covetous, nor drunkards, nor revilers, nor extortioners will inherit the kingdom of God.**

These are some of the things that grieve God's heart; you will see the rest as you go through this book.

In Genesis 6:6, the Bible says "And the Lord was sorry that He had made man on the earth, and He was grieved in His heart." The world is grieving God now by its many acts, which displease Him. God repented creating that male and female he created because of the evil of their heart. This caused God to wipe all the creation through floods, with the exception of one man – Noah, and his family who found grace in the eyes of the Lord.

Noah walked in habitual fellowship with God. Noah had a pure heart that pleased God, and he loved God his creator. Again it is all about the heart. When God searched the earth, He found only one man with a good heart. The rest of mankind corrupted the earth and filled it with violence.

If we look around us now, we would agree that the level of violence in the earth is increasing at an alarming rate. There is no place where you can say you are safe. We are walking around so oblivious, because the devil has blinded us with worldly pleasures. We have polluted the earth again with our sinful nature. When men become lovers of themselves, rather than lovers of God, evil rules in their hearts. The world is dying now because there is no love from a pure heart.

God previously destroyed the whole earth and all the inhabitants of the earth. He only spared Noah and his family because God had seen righteousness before him in Noah's generation.

# 4

# The Restoration of Man to God

**A**FTER the flood it repented the Lord that He had destroyed the earth with flood. So, God vowed He would not curse the ground anymore for man's sake. This shows how much God loved His creation from the beginning. It was not God's intention to destroy the earth and everything that was on it. He had a long-term agenda and it was God's purpose to have everlasting relationship with all creation.

## A merciful and gracious God

We should understand that God, in His infinite mercy, did not destroy man immediately after Adam's disobedience. He gave man a lot of time to work out their relationship with Him. But instead of realigning themselves back to God, men chose to follow their hearts again and chose to love the world more than Him. So it took God 10 generations from Adam, to find a just man like Noah, who would remain after the earth was destroyed.  Noah was a descendant of Seth, so he was Adam's son from the 10th generation.

God made a covenant with Noah and his sons and blessed them and said unto them "Be fruitful and multiply, and fill the earth" (Genesis 9:1). Noah and his sons, in line with this mandate, filled the earth after the flood. As the people multiplied on earth, sin increased on the earth again. Again, people's hearts were turned away from God. Since God had vowed after the flood that He would not destroy man and the earth again with flood, God had to come up with another plan.

God's plan was to find another man on the earth, with whom He would enter a covenant, and build Himself a nation that would serve Him, love Him and keep His commandments. It took another 10 generations after Noah, for Him to find another man, to enter a covenant with. God chose Abram (who became Abraham) to establish a new covenant.

Through Jacob, the son of Isaac and grandson of Abraham, the nation of Israel was born. When the Israelites came out of Egypt, God gave them the Ten Commandments on Mount Sinai, through their leader Moses. These commandments were to help them to have a good relationship with God and each other, and to keep them away from sin. Despite Israel being a chosen nation and being given the Ten Commandments, they still sinned against God and grieved Him. There was a time when God wanted to wipe out all of them in the desert, but Moses intervened and asked God to have mercy.

***And the Lord said to Moses, "Go, get down! For your people whom you brought out of the land of Egypt have corrupted themselves. They have turned***

*aside quickly out of the way which I commanded them. They have made themselves a moulded calf, and worshiped it and sacrificed to it, and said, 'This is your god, O Israel, that brought you out of the land of Egypt!'" And the Lord said to Moses, "I have seen this people, and indeed it is a stiff-necked people! Now therefore, let Me alone, that My wrath may burn hot against them and I may consume them. And I will make of you a great nation." Then Moses pleaded with the Lord his God, and said: "Lord, why does Your wrath burn hot against Your people whom You have brought out of the land of Egypt with great power and with a mighty hand? Why should the Egyptians speak, and say, 'He brought them out to harm them, to kill them in the mountains, and to consume them from the face of the earth'? Turn from Your fierce wrath, and relent from this harm to Your people. Remember Abraham, Isaac, and Israel, Your servants, to whom You swore by Your own self, and said to them, 'I will multiply your descendants as the stars of heaven; and all this land that I have spoken of I give to your descendants, and they shall inherit it forever.'" So the Lord relented from the harm which He said He would do to His people.*

Exodus 32:7–14

The children of Israel grieved God so much that

He wanted to wipe them out, and make Himself a nation out of Moses alone. They murmured and mourned what they were missing in Egypt, and did not appreciate God. Moses' plea to God saved the Israelites from total annihilation. God was grieved with that generation for 40 years, because they disobeyed Him and did not keep His commandments.

In Deuteronomy 6:5, Moses spoke to the children of Israel to love God with all their heart, all their soul and all their mind. Throughout Deuteronomy 6, Moses' emphasis is for the children of Israel to keep the commandments in front of their hearts, not just as a law that was given to them. He asked them to obey, out of love from a pure heart, in order for to maintain good relations with God, and their neighbours.

Despite God's loving mercies and His efforts to keep His relationship with His chosen generation, they grieved Him generation after generation until God sent His begotten Son to die for the world. Jesus did not come to die for the Jews only; He came to die for all of us.

After 42 generations from Abraham, because of God's love for His creation, He sent His only begotten Son to save the world. This was God's last resort to save the dying world. When you read the scripture in John 3:16, you might think that God's love begins from only when He sends His Son to earth; the truth however is that God loved, and has loved the world from the beginning of creation.

The question then is: "What are we doing with God's love?" Many people say they love God but keep on grieving Him. You might ask "How?" or "When?" It is pertinent to ask these questions. In all honesty, we need to divorce the world, and its attributes. Then we need to fall in love with Jesus our Saviour, as He is our unifier with God.

# 5

# The Ten Commandments

**J**ESUS Christ, in Matthew 22:36-40, gives a summary of the commandments after He was asked which was the greatest commandment. Love was and still is the greatest commandment.

When the children of Israel came out of Egypt, God gave Moses the Ten Commandments on Mount Sinai. If you look at these commandments in Exodus 20:1-17, you will notice that God gave them these commandments in order to save them from sinning. The Ten Commandments were given to maintain a good relationship with God, and also for man to have good relationships with one another. God wanted a nation that would love Him and obey Him by keeping His commandments. In the first four commandments God speaks about himself:

*I am the Lord your God, who brought you out of the land of Egypt, out of the house of bondage. "And God spoke all these words, saying: "I am the Lord your God, who brought you out of the land of Egypt, out of the house of bondage. "You shall have no other gods before Me. "You*

**shall not make for yourself a carved image—any likeness of anything that is in heaven above, or that is in the earth beneath, or that is in the water under the earth; you shall not bow down to them nor serve them. For I, the Lord your God, am a jealous God, visiting the iniquity of the fathers upon the children to the third and fourth generations of those who hate Me, but showing mercy to thousands, to those who love Me and keep My commandments. "You shall not take the name of the Lord your God in vain, for the Lord will not hold him guiltless who takes His name in vain. "Remember the Sabbath day, to keep it holy. Six days you shall labour and do all your work, but the seventh day is the Sabbath of the Lord your God. In it you shall do no work: you, nor your son, nor your daughter, nor your male servant, nor your female servant, nor your cattle, nor your stranger who is within your gates. For in six days the Lord made the heavens and the earth, the sea, and all that is in them, and rested the seventh day. Therefore the Lord blessed the Sabbath day and hallowed it.**

Exodus 20:2–11

The fifth commandment says "Honour your father and your mother, that your days may be long upon the land which the Lord your God is giving you." The fifth commandment speaks about honouring your father and mother, because they are the people that will teach you the law and the statutes of God. Your parents will also guide you through life and be influential in your upbringing. So honour and not humiliate them.

> **"And these words which I command you today shall be in your heart. You shall teach them diligently to your children, and shall talk of them when you sit in your house, when you walk by the way, when you lie down, and when you rise up."**
>
> Deuteronomy 6:6–7

When God gave them these commandments, He spoke of Himself (God) and our neighbour. The reason was that most of the time we sin against God, and we sin with our neighbour. As we have seen, God speaks about Himself in the first four commandments, and then speaks about the neighbour in the rest:

> **"You shall not murder. You shall not commit adultery. You shall not steal. You shall not bear false witness against your neighbour. You shall not covet your neighbour's house; you shall not covet your neighbour's wife, nor his male servant, nor his female servant, nor his ox, nor his donkey, nor anything that is your neighbour's."**
>
> Exodus 20:13–17

Therefore the second greatest commandment is: 'You shall love your neighbour as yourself (Matthew 22:39). If you love your neighbour as yourself you will not harm or hurt your neighbour.

## Who is your neighbour?

In Luke 10: 25-37 Jesus also explains who the neighbour is.

> *And behold, a certain lawyer stood up and tested Him, saying, "Teacher, what shall I do to inherit eternal life?" He said to him, "What is written in the law? What is your reading of it?" So he answered and said, "'You shall love the Lord your God with all your heart, with all your soul, with all your strength, and with all your mind,' and 'your neighbour as yourself.'" And He said to him, "You have answered rightly; do this and you will live." But he, wanting to justify himself, said to Jesus, "And who is my neighbour?" Then Jesus answered and said: "A certain man went down from Jerusalem to Jericho, and fell among thieves, who stripped him of his clothing, wounded him, and departed, leaving him half dead. Now by chance a certain priest came down that road. And when he saw him, he passed by on the other side. Likewise a Levite, when he arrived at the place, came and looked, and passed by on the other side. But a certain Samaritan, as he journeyed, came where he was. And when he saw him, he*

*had compassion. So he went to him and bandaged his wounds, pouring on oil and wine; and he set him on his own animal, brought him to an inn, and took care of him. On the next day, when he departed, he took out two denarii, gave them to the innkeeper and said to him, 'Take care of him; and whatever more you spend, when I come again, I will repay you.' So which of these three do you think was neighbour to him who fell among the thieves?" And he said, "He who showed mercy on him." Then Jesus said to him, "Go and do likewise."*

Your neighbour is not only the person who lives next door. Your neighbour is anyone and everyone with whom you come in contact - on the bus, in the street, on the train, at your workplace, gym, church, and shops.

How many people today, stop to help others in need? In the story told by Jesus, we see that even the priest and the Levite, who both knew about God, walked past the wounded man without helping him. They passed him, because they did not know him. He was a stranger to them, he didn't fellowship with them, and he was not a member in their church. They had never seen him before, and he was not their relative.

I have personally witnessed so many sad incidents of people's behaviour towards the poor and the needy. On one occasion, I was having lunch in a restaurant in Zimbabwe, and a lady waked in carrying a child on her back. The child was about four years-old, and disabled. This woman came to beg for money in a restaurant, full of diners tucking into their burgers and chips, and laughing away at the same time. No one paid attention to this lady, or her child. I was shocked!

I watched this situation for about five minutes. But nobody paid any attention to the lady. So, I stood up, approached the lady and gave her some money. It was after I did this, that I actually found out that her child was disabled, and they had no money to eat. The child could not walk, and she was unable to afford a wheelchair. I was touched by her plight, but I was also angry that no one else in that restaurant had paid her any attention. They had no love in their hearts to give to the lady; they couldn't feel her pain. Where is the love?

Unfortunately, I was so overwhelmed by the lady's plight that I forgot to take her address to see what could be done about helping her to get a wheelchair for her son.

The above account is not an isolated event. I have come across so many similar scenarios. How many of us have done the same thing, as the Levite and the priest who walked past a stranger who clearly needed help? Some people have so many pairs of shoes and bags, and some live in posh houses and drive Porsche cars. But they don't care about the dying world. We are always buying new clothes, yet there is someone out there just looking for a meal. Some children are working as sex-slaves, just to make a living for themselves and their families. Do you feel affected when you watch news and documentaries about these children? Do you do anything about it? Where is the love?

My heart sank when I watched a documentary about how some rich men travel to Zambia, to sexually abuse young boys. I started thinking that the hearts of these men are callous. Instead of abuse them as they did, why would these men not give these children a home and offer them a better life? In my opinion, there should be no street-kids in any country, as long as there are people rich enough to take these children into their homes.

We learn from this, that if we do not love our neighbour, the love of God is not in us. We ought to love our neighbour as ourselves. God expects us to look out for each other, and take care of each other, as the Good Samaritan did. We are not supposed to help only those we know. We should help everyone we meet, who needs help. The word 'LOVE' is not just a four letter word; it is the one that is key to the entire creation.

The commandments of God do not just enable us to build a strong relationship with God our Creator; they also help us to build strong relationships with one another. This book is written for both believers and unbelievers. To those who are not familiar with the Word of God, I would like to mention at this point that, although the Ten Commandments were given to the children of Israel then, the commandments also apply to us today.

For you to enjoy or experience the love of God you need to give your life to God by inviting the Lord

Jesus Christ into your life. I truly believe that by the time you finish reading this book, your life will not be the same, and you will begin to experience the true love of God. You will also be able to share with others, the true love of God.

If you have not given your life to Jesus Christ, and you feel that at this point you want to surrender your life to Him, I would like to invite you to pray this prayer of confession and invite Him into your life.

'Dear Jesus I confess that you are my Lord and Personal Saviour.

I believe in my heart that you died and rose again.

Father, forgive me of all my sins and cleanse me from all unrighteousness.

Come into my life today and come in to stay. Amen.'

*That if you confess with your mouth the Lord Jesus and believe in your heart that God has raised Him from the dead, you will be saved.*

Romans 10:9

*If we say that we have no sin, we deceive ourselves, and the truth is not in us. If we confess our sins, He is faithful and just to forgive us our sins and to cleanse us from all unrighteous-*

***ness. If we say that we have not sinned,
we make Him a liar, and His word is not
in us.***

1 John 1:8-10

If you have confessed Jesus Christ as your Lord and personal Saviour, you are now saved. This means that you have access to the throne of grace to ask God for anything. I have broken the prayer of salvation into two parts to make people understand that we have to confess Him first and believe that He died for us before we can ask Him to forgive our sins. When He has cleansed you He will then give you the Holy Spirit.

If you have prayed this prayer genuinely with faith in your heart, you are now born-again. What you need to do is to find a good church, where you can fellowship with others, and be fed the Word of God. You will also be baptised in water, and in the Holy Ghost. The prayer of salvation is also at the back of this book if you want to use it to help others come to the knowledge of God and His dear Son Jesus Christ.

∞ ∞ ∞

We must remember that even Jesus came through love, and became a servant of God. He came to obey the law perfectly in our place so that we could be counted as righteous. He came to die on the Cross to take the curse of the law in our place. Jesus Christ lived a perfect life, but He had to sacrifice His life by dying for us, and fulfilling the law once and for all. In our lives Jesus has fulfilled this law as the Holy Spirit teaches us, convicts us, and matures us daily through His Word. When our obedience flows from hearing the Word of God, we will have a new heart through the love of God which is in Christ Jesus. Love and the commandments that we obey are centred on Jesus Christ, and our membership in heaven as Christians will be secured after we have learnt how to love each other with the love of God. Love therefore, is the key to eternal life.

Christ obeys the law perfectly in our place:

> *Let this mind be in you which was also in Christ Jesus, who, being in the form of God, did not consider it robbery to be equal with God, but made Himself of no reputation, taking the form of a bondservant, and coming in the likeness of men. And being found in appearance as a man, He humbled Himself and became obedient to the point of death, even the death of the cross. Therefore God also has highly exalted Him and given Him the name which is above every name, that at the name of Jesus every knee should bow, of those in heaven, and of those on earth, and of those under the earth, and that every tongue should confess that Jesus Christ is Lord, to the glory of God the Father.*
>
> Philippians 2:5-11

Loving God and keeping His commandments is like cleaning your house with bleach and disinfectant. It helps you to stay away from sin, and it opens up your mind which has been blinded by the world's propaganda.

> *But even if our gospel is veiled, it is veiled to those who are perishing, whose minds the god of this age has blinded, who do not believe, lest the light of the gospel of the glory of Christ, who is the image of God, should shine on them.*

> 2 Corinthians 4:3-4

The devil blinds the minds of people and their hearts, so that they cannot know God and His love. The enemy wants to keep us in bondage, so that we will be his servants. He likes sending us to do his errands, because he cannot do them himself. Can you imagine being the servant of the devil, running up down to do his bidding? Such a person is blinded by earthly things that perish and have no eternal value. But, when we love God and keep His commandments, we know that we know Him and we walk in perfect love. He (God) daily leads us in the path of righteousness for His name sake.

> *For this is the love of God, that we keep His commandments. And His commandments are not burdensome.*
> 1 John 5:3

Our love for one another is measured by our loving God, and keeping His commandments. God wants us to keep His commandments because they are not grievous. We need to capitalise on this love for us to mature in the Lord and have eternal life.

# 6

# The Source of God's Love

**I**N 1 John 4:7-21, Apostle John writes about the love of God and its source. The source of the love of God is Jesus Christ as we can read in verses 9 – 10: In this the love of God was manifested toward us, that God has sent His only begotten Son into the world, that we might live through Him. In this is love, not that we loved God, but that He loved us and sent His Son to be the propitiation for our sins.

This is the gift of love that God has given to the whole world for free and unconditionally. It is good to know that God loves us so much. What do we do with this great love that God has bestowed upon us? The answer should be 'We have to love him too'. Our love for God is measured by how much we keep His commandments, and love one another.

> *Beloved, let us love one another, for love is of God; and everyone who loves is born of God and knows God.*
>
> 1 John 4:7

The key message here is for us to love God and to love one another with the love of God.

*Beloved, if God so loved us, we also ought to love one another.*

1 John 4:11

If the perfect love of God is in us, how then can we hate one another? How do we keep malice with one another? How come we do not speak to one another, because we don't fellowship in the same church, speak the same language, have the same skin colour, belong to the same denomination, or come from the same country? When we become born-again, the love of God is in us, and it binds us together. Our differences should not matter, 'For there is one God, One Lord, and one Spirit.'

**He who says he is in the light, and hates his brother, is in darkness until now. He who loves his brother abides in the light, and there is no cause for stumbling in him. But he who hates his brother is in darkness and walks in darkness, and does not know where he is going, because the darkness has blinded his eyes.**

1 John 2:9-11

So how many of us in the Body of Christ are walking in darkness? How many murderers are in the house of God? Are you one of them? If you have a grudge, or you have malice or strife against your brethren, you are a murderer. Churches are full, yet there are so many 'believers' still walking in darkness because they don't love their brothers. We can never say we love God if we don't love one another. You don't have to carry a gun or a knife to be a murderer. This is deep and may be uncomfortable; when you don't love your brother you are a murderer.

I believe that if we are truly born-again, our attitudes towards God and towards one another will change. Our behaviour must change because God has given us His Spirit. He dwells in us, and we dwell in Him. We become new, and we keep His commandments. If we love God with all our hearts, mind and soul there will be no room for evil, because God dwells in us and God is love.

*The Spirit of truth, whom the world cannot receive, because it neither sees Him nor knows Him; but you know Him, for He dwells with you and will be in you. I will not leave you orphans; I will come to you. "A little while longer and the world will see Me no more, but you will see Me. Because I live, you will live also. At that day you will know that I am in My Father, and you in Me, and I in you. He who has My commandments and keeps them, it is he who loves Me. And he who loves Me will be loved by My Father, and I will love him and manifest Myself to him." Judas (not Iscariot) said to Him, "Lord, how is it that You will manifest Yourself to us, and not to the world?" Jesus answered and said to him,*

*"**If anyone loves Me, he will keep My word; and My Father will love him, and We will come to him and make Our home with him. He who does not love Me does not keep My words; and the word which you hear is not Mine but the Father's who sent Me.***

John 14:17-23

We can see that Jesus Christ again, mentions the keeping of commandments and loving Him and His Father. So, we cannot keep God's commandments without loving Him.

# 7

# Guard Your Heart

**T**HE heart is an engine that controls our behaviour. This is why the Bible says we should guard our hearts.

*Keep your heart with all diligence, for out it spring the issues of life.*
Proverbs 4:23

*For from within, out of the heart of men, proceed evil thoughts, adulteries, fornications, murders.*
Mark 7:21

*A good man out of the good treasure of his heart brings forth good; and an evil man out of the evil treasure of his heart brings forth evil. For out of the abundance of the heart his mouth speaks.*

*Luke 6:45*

As we can see from these scriptures, the heart is the key element in our walks of life. The heart speaks volumes and it degrades humankind.

*Then the Lord saw that the wickedness of man was great in the earth, and that every intent of the thoughts of his heart was only evil continually. And the Lord was sorry that He had made man on the earth, and He was grieved in His heart. So the Lord said, "I will destroy man whom I have created from the face of the earth, both man and beast, creeping thing and birds of the air, for I am sorry that I have made them." But Noah found grace in the eyes of the Lord.*

Genesis 6:6-8

It is the heart of man that caused God to destroy the entire earth, apart from Noah and his family, with the flood. God saw Noah's heart, and was prepared to start a new generation without sin. He wanted an earth full of people like Noah that would love Him, and not the world. Our hearts can deceive us by making us long for things that are not beneficial to us; things that would rather destroy us. Without the love of God in our hearts, we are bound to make foolish mistakes that could cost us our lives.

*But know this, that in the last days perilous times will come: For men will be lovers of themselves, lovers of money, boasters, proud, blasphemers, disobedient to parents, unthankful, unholy, unloving, unforgiving, slanderers, with-*

***out self-control, brutal, despisers of good, traitors, headstrong, haughty, lovers of pleasure rather than lovers of God.***

2 Timothy 3:1-4

These scriptures sum up what happens when we turn our hearts from God; we become lovers of the world that is full of evil and corruption. We now allow our hearts to rule us as it happened in the time of Noah, and later in Sodom and Gomorrah.

***The heart is deceitful above all things, And desperately wicked; Who can know it?***

Jeremiah 17: 9

***For from within, out of the heart of men, proceed evil thoughts, adulteries, fornications, murders.***

Mark 7:21

How then do we guard our hearts? Simply by giving our hearts to the Lord - by loving God with all our hearts, all our mind, all our might and all our soul; and by loving our neighbours as ourselves, and by keeping all God's commandments (Matthew 22:36–40).

You will come across this scripture throughout this book because it is the main guideline for our lives. As we have seen in the previous chapters, after creation God saw that the earth and everything in it were beautiful, including humans. If we look at the earth today, everything still looks beautiful - the animals, the rivers, the valleys, the mountains, the trees, and every other aspect of God's creation - except the violence on the earth caused by mankind.

We have made the earth so unbearable to live in through wars, greed, pride, hatred, bitterness, malice, envy, hurting one another, stealing from one another and covetousness. Families are falling apart; there is hatred among siblings. Quarrels, unforgiveness and malice have become the order of the day simply because there is no love of God in people's hearts. Marriages are breaking down, because there is no love of God in the hearts of husbands and wives. Church members are fighting each other, and churches are splitting up because there is no love of God in people's hearts. Wars rage around the world, terrorism is on the rise, there are gangs in our schools and communities, and vandalism thrives because there is no love of God in the hearts of people.

Through all these things, we have polluted the earth and departed from the original intention of God. Jesus Christ our Saviour is the only Way to restore us to our Creator. He shed His blood on the Cross of Calvary for our sins. In other words, Jesus shed His blood to cleanse the mess we created on earth after turning away from God and His commandments. We thank God that through His love and His infinite mercy He gave His begotten Son to die on the Cross, so that we can be reconciled to Him. This love of God will be explored in the following chapters.

# 8

# Rooted and Grounded in Love

**I** **WOULD** like to emphasize that we all need to look into our hearts. This is important even if you are born-again, or have been attending church from a very young age. Sometimes when there is an altar-call, people run out to give their lives to Christ. What usually happens is that these people run to the front, but leave their hearts behind. So, they do not totally surrender their hearts to the Lord. Some others believe in the Lord Jesus, because of the miracles they crave or see, and are not totally sold out to God. In time, they become church-goers, or backslide completely. Without their hearts being involved, these people are not rooted and grounded in love with Christ Jesus.

> *That Christ may dwell in your hearts through faith; that you, being rooted and grounded in love.*
>
> Ephesians 3:17

When we are rooted and grounded in love, we become passionate about our God. We walk more closely with Him, and understand Him better. This helps us to build a one-to-one relationship with God, and also helps us to build a healthy relationship with one another.

The love of God is not like the love the world gives; one minute the world loves you, the next minute, you are their number one enemy. The people of the world can promise you all the love in the world, but when you have a misunderstanding with them, they will curse you.  Unlike men, God loves you always.

We learnt that Jesus did not commit Himself to the multitude that followed Him after they saw the miracles because He knew the nature of man's heart (John 2: 23-25). Jesus Christ knew that they were not there for Him, but were only there to receive the miracles. It happens today – some people only want to be around certain people, or around us, because of what they can get. Some will even come in the name of love. This is why it is important to have the love of God in our hearts.

I once counselled a lady who was hurting so much because a man had deceived her. She had fallen in love with this man when she went on holiday to Africa, but the man had something else up his sleeves. On her return to England they made plan for him to join her later, and he did. When the man arrived in England, he told the lady he wanted to study, so they would have a better future together. He consequently enrolled at a university course outside London, while the lady continued to live in London. The lady was responsible for all his expenses, including school fees. She did this faithfully for three years, until he graduated.

The man got the lady pregnant during that time, and also talked the lady into building a house in Africa, which she did. When the man completed his studies, he told the lady that he wanted them to return to Africa and settle down there. The plan was that he would go first, and sort out things for the lady and their daughter to join him later. Three months after he left, communication between the lady and the man began to be less frequent, and she began to suspect foul play. When she questioned him about plans for her relocation to Africa with their daughter, the man would offer one excuse or the other. Eventually, the lady decided to travel to Africa with her daughter, only to find out that the man had married all along, and was living with another woman in the house that she had built.

Sadly, the word 'love' is continuously being abused throughout the world. This woman's experience is not an isolated one and I have come across many similar scenarios – men deceiving women, and vice versa. Some men (or women) would not just leave you to be with somebody else; they will also kill so they can get you out of their life. In my counselling sessions with the woman, I made her see reasons she should be thankful to God. I told her that God takes away pain, and that she should forgive the man and take everything to the Lord in prayer. I reassured her that God will answer her in due course.

In Matthew 15:7-8, Jesus Christ talks about people who draw near to Him with their mouth, but their hearts stay far from Him.

*Hypocrites! Well did Isaiah prophesy about you, saying: 'These people draw near to Me with their mouth, And honour Me with their lips, But their heart is far from Me.*

Matthew 15:7–8

We ought to remember that miracles are the demonstration of the power of God. If we come to God because we have a need, when our needs are met, we will forget God until another need arises. I have seen it happen so many times - when some people get their breakthroughs, they become part-time lovers of God.

I remember a gentleman who had immigration problems, and was actually about to be deported from the United Kingdom. This man was so zealous in church during this period. He never missed Bible studies, night vigils, or Sunday services. He was so committed, that he would also stay behind to help in the church, and he would even clean the toilet. When his immigration matter was sorted out, he started skipping services and eventually stopped coming to church. When the pastor asked him why he no longer attended church services, he said he was working and had no time. This man suddenly forgot the God who gave him the papers that permitted him to work.

There are a lot of people who are in the house of God now, because they are troubled by one thing or another. It is important to love God for who He is and not for what He can do for us.

We need to stop using God. We should first love Him as He first loved us. God wants genuine love from us, not what we can get from Him. When we love God with all our hearts, mind, and soul, it will be so easy for us to know and understand Him.

# 9

# Walking In Love

**T**HE Christian life demands diligence, careful and persistent application of effort in pursuing moral excellence, knowledge, self-control, perseverance, godliness, brotherly love, kindness, and selfless love. These are the ingredients needed to be effective Christians. The most vital ingredient is brotherly love. God wants us to walk in love so as to fulfil the law.

> *Therefore be imitators of God as dear children. And walk in love, as Christ also has loved us and given Himself for us, an offering and a sacrifice to God for a sweet-smelling aroma.*
>
> Ephesians 5: 1-2

There is a stench on our streets today. We have polluted our streets with our sins. The Bible tells us to walk in love because love is a powerful broom to sweep away the mess that our sins have created (Ephesians 5:1). Jesus Christ our Saviour gave Himself for us as a sweet-smelling sacrifice to God. When we give our hearts to the Lord, loving Him with all our heart, soul, and mind, we are cleansed from our filthy state.

> *Be kindly affectionate to one another with brotherly love, in honour giving preference to one another.*
>
> Romans 12:10

We need to be kind to, and forgive one another. Being Christians does not mean that we will not have differences. But we have the advantage of knowing that the Word of God is there to direct us to resolve any differences. There should be a difference in the way differences are handled by believers, compared to how situations are handled by those who are not born-again. First of all, brotherly love should be a key element in resolving misunderstandings amongst believers. We have been mentioning the word 'love' throughout this book because love is so important.

The word of God says in Colossians 3:12 that we are to 'Put on therefore, as the elect of God, holy and beloved, bowels of mercies, kindness, humbleness of mind, meekness, longsuffering.' (KJV) Bowels of mercies indicates being able to forgive 70 X 7 times.

> *Then Peter came to Him and said, "Lord, how often shall my brother sin against me, and I forgive him? Up to seven times?" Jesus said to him, "I do not say*

*to you, up to seven times, but up to seventy times seven.*

Matthew 18:21-22

*But if you have bitter envy and self-seeking in your hearts, do not boast and lie against the truth.*

James 3:14

*Finally, all of you be of one mind, having compassion for one another; love as brothers, be tender-hearted, be courteous.*

1 Peter 3: 8

# 10

# What Is Love?

**SO** what is love? The definition of love that God wants us to have is in 1 Corinthians 13:4-7. Love suffers long, and it is having patience with imperfect people. Love is kind and active in doing good. Love does not envy, since it is non-possessive and non-competitive. Love actually wants other people to get ahead. Hence it does not parade itself. Love is not puffed up, or treats others arrogantly.

It does not behave rudely, but displays good manners and courtesy. Love does not seek its own, insisting on its own rights and demanding precedence, rather, it is unselfish. Love is not easily provoked, it is not irritable or touchy, rough or hostile, but is graceful under pressure.

Love does not think evil or keep record of evil. Love does not rejoice in iniquity or find satisfaction in the short comings of others. Love is not involved in the spreading an evil report; rather, it rejoices in the truth, and aggressively advertises the good in others. Love bears all things and concerns itself in defending and holding other people up. Love believes all things, thinks the best about others, credits them with good intentions, and is not suspicious. Love hopes all things, is never giving up on people, but affirming their future. Love endures all things persevering and remaining loyal to the end.

> *Though I speak with the tongues of men and of angels, but have not love, I have become sounding brass or a clanging cymbal. And though I have the gift of prophecy, and understand all mysteries and all knowledge, and though I have all faith, so that I could remove mountains, but have not love, I am nothing. And though I bestow all my goods to feed the poor, and though I give my body to be burned, but have not love, it profits me nothing. Love suffers long and is kind; love does not envy; love does not parade itself, is not puffed up; does not behave rudely, does not seek its own, is not provoked, thinks no evil; does not rejoice in iniquity, but rejoices in the truth; bears all things, believes all things, hopes all things, endures all things. Love never fails. But whether there are prophecies, they will fail; whether there are tongues, they will cease; whether there is knowledge, it will vanish away. For we know in part and we prophesy in part. But when that which is perfect has come, then that which is in part will be done away. When I was a child, I spoke as a child, I understood as a child, I*

> *thought as a child; but when I became a man, I put away childish things. For now we see in a mirror, dimly, but then face to face. Now I know in part, but then I shall know just as I also am known. And now abide faith, hope, love, these three; but the greatest of these is love.*
>
> 1 Corinthians 13:1-13

From the first three verses of 1 Corinthians 13, we learn that gifts, in contrast to love, are partial and incomplete. They are temporal, not eternal; they communicate imperfect rather than perfect knowledge. We also learn that even if we are considered to be spiritually gifted, without the love, it profits us nothing.

> *Though I speak with the tongues of men and of angels, but have not love, I have become sounding brass or a clanging cymbal. And though I have the gift of prophecy, and understand all mysteries and all knowledge, and though I have all faith, so that I could remove mountains, but have not love, I am nothing. And though I bestow all my goods to feed the poor, and though I give my body to be burned, but have not love, it profits me nothing.*
>
> 1 Corinthians 13:1-3

Some of us are carried away by the demonstration of spiritual gifts. We forget that gifts come from

God. Love however, comes from our hearts. You can have a gift of healing and be used of God to heal all manner of diseases and sicknesses; without love, it profits you nothing. You can have a gift of miracles and be seen to perform various kinds of miracles; without love, it profits you nothing. You may be able to cast out devils, and be seen as a deliverance guru; without love, it profits you nothing. You can also lead Praise and Worship sessions in church and bring down the anointing of God; without love, it profits you nothing. Whatever the gifts, without love, the result will be the same – there will be no profit. Gifts are demonstrations of the power of God, so we need to play our part by fulfilling the law of love.

> **And when He had called His twelve disciples to Him, He gave them power over unclean spirits, to cast them out, and to heal all kinds of sickness and all kinds of disease.**
>
> Matthew 10:1

If this law of love is not fulfilled our work will be in vain when He comes, and we will be counted unworthy.

> **"Not everyone who says to Me, 'Lord, Lord,' shall enter the kingdom of heaven, but he who does the will of My Father in heaven. Many will say to Me in that day, 'Lord, Lord, have we not prophesied in**

***Your name, cast out demons in Your name, and done many wonders in Your name?' And then I will declare to them, 'I never knew you; depart from Me, you who practice lawlessness!'***

Matthew 7:21-23

***If you really fulfill the royal law according to the Scripture, "You shall love your neighbour as yourself," you do well.***

James 2:8

Therefore, love is the fulfilling of the law.

# 11

# A Callous Heart

**W**HEN there is no love of God in the heart of a man, it will be callous. There is no good feeling at all in the heart of a man who does not love his neighbour. One day, I watched a documentary about women in Congo who had been raped repeatedly by soldiers. My heart went out to those women. I just wanted to get on an aeroplane to them, to let them know how much Jesus loved them. I just felt that they needed love and understanding to overcome their nightmares. Only Jesus can heal the emotional, mental, psychological and physical scars that those women were left with. In that documentary the soldiers did not show any remorse at all, because there was no love in their hearts. The men's hearts were full of evil and venom. They needed Jesus in their hearts.

If Jesus is in your heart, evil will not prevail. Our main scripture in Matthew 22: 36-40, tells us to 'Love God with all our heart, mind, and soul; and to love our neighbour as ourselves. No one wants anything bad to happen to them. If you love your neighbour as yourself, with the love of God, you will not harm your neighbour.

The wickedness that those soldiers perpetrated against the women they raped, stemmed from evil hearts - hearts that did not know anything but violence. The political system and order in their country had failed them, violence and hatred were all they had been taught. Their hearts had gone so cold, that they had become emotionless. To combat this problem, the love of God must be preached throughout the nations. Congo is not the only country facing such problems; the whole world is in turmoil. There is currently a lot of abuse and violence in this world, and no law besides the law of God, can stop it.

It may be easy to argue that in Congo for instance, people are suffering because there are no effective laws. But even in some countries where there are effective laws, when it comes to issues like rape, you will agree that there is not much difference.

In countries where law is effective to some extent, there are still major problems, because people go through violent attacks. People are physically and emotionally abused. There are serial killers, criminal gangs, suicide bombers, and gang rapists prowling the streets. Prison sentences, summary executions, and even death penalties have not provided the necessary solutions. Legal dispositions have only afforded us short-term relief, rather than permanent answers.

Sometimes in countries with enforceable laws, perpetrators are caught and put in prison to serve their sentences. But what happens when the sentence is completed? They are released back into the society, where they go on to commit crime, again and again. What does this tell us? The prison only punishes the flesh; it will never punish the heart or the spirit in that person. This is the reason that people re-offend, after being released from prison.

Prisons all over the world are full to their capacities, yet some countries are experiencing a large increase in the number of people re-offending. This simply tells us that no human system can change any human being; we have to return to the laws of God. We have to know and love God first, as He was the one who instituted these laws in the first place. When we can keep His laws of love, we will be able to keep the rest of the commandments. Remember, "The heart is deceitful above all things, And desperately wicked; Who can know it?" (Jeremiah 17:9).

> *For from within, out of the heart of men, proceed evil thoughts, adulteries, forni-cations, murders, thefts, covetousness, wickedness, deceit, lewdness, an evil eye, blasphemy, pride, foolishness. All these evil things come from within and defile a man."*
>
> Mark 7:21-23

Before a person physically commits any sin, it is first conceived in the heart. For example, before a person steals, the heart longs for that item. If somebody is desperate for an expensive car or lifestyle that they can't afford, the next thing they will do is to steal to satisfy their heart's desire. Their heart sends a signal to the mind. The mind will then work hard to execute it by coming up with plans to obtain the money, or to steal the car or other items outright. The heart longs, and the mind executes it.

In a similar manner, before a man rapes a woman, his heart first lust after her. The next step is for the mind to execute a plan for how and when the rape will take place. There are so many examples we can consider, which can destroy a person, because of the content and intent of the heart.

> *Since you have purified your souls in obeying the truth through the Spirit in sincere love of the brethren, love one another fervently with a pure heart.*

> 1 Peter 1:22

Let us also remember that if we have envy, strife, malice, unforgiveness, and anger towards one another, we are sinners. The love of God is not in us. Our behaviour and attitudes towards one another must be Christ-like, as we are the salt of this world.

# 12

# Provocation and Silent Killers

**W**HEN we become born-again we learn a different way to deal with offences when they come our way. Ephesians 4: 26-27 talks about us getting angry with one another and resolving the issue amicably. The longer we leave a situation unresolved, the worse it gets. It could lead to malice and strife. The time-scale the Bible gives us to sort out our differences is by sunset, so that we don't give place to the devil. Nothing good that comes out of our mouths when we are angry. This is because our hearts will be bitter and we will think evil. So the best thing to do is to pray, then call the person involved and sort out the differences.

> *"Be angry, and do not sin": do not let the sun go down on your wrath, nor give place to the devil.*
>
> Ephesians 4:26-27

Some people think when they become born-again, they will not face provocation, and that life will be a bed of roses. But the truth is that offences will come. The good news however is that when offences come, the Word of God and the love of God in us are there to help us to deal the pain and hurt. The love of God that is put into our hearts helps us to overcome trials, tribulations and temptations and resolve our differences. God's love helps us to relate one to another in a humble way. It stops us living in malice, strife and hatred.

One thing we should always remember is that we don't have to be at fault for us to be reproached, or to be offended by others. You may even be offended by people who are very close to you. Those whom you least expect to do you wrong, are the ones that will do terrible things, and even rub it in your face. It is more hurtful when the act is carried out by someone you truly care about, or a person that you have done so much for.

When someone you helped turns round and stabs you in the back, your first response is likely to be 'I don't want to see him or her again!' You want to eradicate them from your life. This is normal for every human being. I have come across some people of the same family who have not spoken to each other for 30 years or more, because of their differences. These family members had vowed never to speak to each other for as long as they lived!

A happy home is one where the love of God is present. When there is a problem, the family members should turn to God in prayer and remind each other of the Word of God. When there is no love of God or the knowledge of the true nature of the Creator, the way people approach their problems is to engage in malice and avoid each other. They may even pass this anomaly from one generation to the next, unless Jesus Christ intervenes. But if the love of God was in them, they will act differently towards each other.

∞∞∞

## Silent killers

When people talk about you and fabricate falsehood, fear sets in. You become fearful of what people are thinking about you, and how they are going to look at you. Hatred creeps in, because of what people are saying. You may even become resentful. You have sleepless nights, you start to worry, and feel defenceless. Some people end up having nervous breakdowns because of such experiences. There are people going through similar experience, or who are struggling with depression right now. My prayer is that the Lord Jesus Christ will bring the much needed healing into their lives today.

People don't only murder people by strangulation or the use of knives and guns. There are a lot of murderers in the society, who cut others down with their razor-sharp tongues. I call them 'silent killers'. These are the tale-bearers, the pathological liars, and the gossips who specialise in creating confusion and straining cordial relationships. These 'silent killers' go about destroying people's lives, and turning everyone they know against them.

It is so difficult when people malign your name because you are forever trying to defend yourself.

The more you try to try defend yourself, the more they attempt to incriminate you. When you are on the receiving end of false accusation, it destroys your reputation and your confidence.

Some people have such a serpentine tongue, that when they lie against you, everyone believes them. You can't win against them. It takes some serious prayers and deliverance to be free from their lies. I was a victim of this until I became born-again and received my deliverance. People used to constantly lie against me, and I was constantly defending myself. On one occasion my manager lied against me, and I lost my job. This makes you wonder how many people out there have lost their jobs, their marriages and their families just because of lies told blatantly by one individual.

Some people feel like they can only be recognised when they put others down, or by make them to look stupid. They want to be in the limelight, and they want to be more recognised at the expense of others. They will do anything to get this recognition, whether it hurts others or not. Their victims are left with emotional scars, and fear, such that it takes the grace of God to come out. People behave this way because the love of God is not in them. They have a callous heart!

I found out that there are people who still do this to others even when they say there are born-again. This shows that people can be born-again by mouth, not from their heart. They wear their Jesus on the outside, but not in their heart. But as born-again

Christians, we need to show good examples to people in the world, of how to behave towards one another. We can only do this by loving one another from and with a pure heart.

# Testimonies

**W**HEN I was ministering to a congregation in Zimbabwe, there was a young lady whom the Holy Spirit drew me to. The Holy Spirit revealed to me that the lady had tried to commit suicide three times. I called the lady to come forward; and when I asked her why she wanted to commit suicide, she said it was because people were mocking her for being ugly. This woman had been called 'ugly' since she was young and that made her lose confidence in herself.

I then asked the lady to turn around and face the congregation, who were astonished, because she did not look ugly at all. This young lady had lost her self-esteem; she felt nobody loved her, and she was crying for help. What she needed was the true love from God, and a genuine love from brethren.

Who gave us such rights over each other? Definitely not God. The world teaches us to discriminate, but the Bible teaches us to 'esteem others better than ourselves'.

*Therefore if there is any consolation in Christ, if any comfort of love, if any fellowship of the Spirit, if any affection and mercy, fulfill my joy by being like-minded, having the same love, being of one accord, of one mind. Let nothing be done through selfish ambition or conceit, but in lowliness of mind let each esteem others better than himself. Let each of you look out not only for his own interests, but also for the interests of others.*

Philippians 2:1-4

*Be kindly affectionate to one another with brotherly love, in honour giving preference to one another.*

Romans 12:10

I told the lady I was ministering to that God loves her, Jesus loves her and that I love her with the love of God. I reassured her that she was beautiful, and I gave her a big hug. After the service, I prayed for her and ministered deliverance - cancelling all the negatives words that had been pronounced on her, and cast out the spirit of rejection. The Lord delivered her. When she came to the service the following day, she looked amazing. She walked in confidently, with a big smile on her face.

That lady is one of the thousands of people that I have come across in my ministry, who have been hurt in their lives. Some have been hurt by their parents, and these hurts have followed them everywhere. I met another lady who was bullied at school, and called 'fat' by her own mother. She also tried to commit suicide several times as a result. Thank God for Jesus, that she is alive today and strong in the faith. She is now offering counselling to other people and encouraging them in the Lord.

Another lady that I met was abused by her mother mentally, emotionally and physically. She was bullied in school, and was sexually abused at the age of seven. This young woman could not sit among people and have a straight forward conversation because of fear of rejection. When I first met her, she did not talk much until she got used to me. When I got to know her, I learnt a great deal about what she had gone through. My heart was sobbing. We prayed together, and the Lord Almighty delivered her from fear and rejection. She is a pastor today and ready to launch her own ministry. Glory be to God.

The world is full of people who are depressed as a result of degradation, and this can sink someone's life. Abused women tend to end up in wrong relationships because of low self-esteem. I have also met a lot of men who have been put down and who suffer from low self-esteem. Many have tried to commit suicide several times. Some have joined gangs to fit in; some do not have wives because they can't even talk to women, as they feel inferior.

I have found out that people that suffer from insecurities, tend to be taken advantage of by those they love and trust. How many people do you know who suffer from insecurities and inferiority complex? And how many have you helped? Are you the one that laughs and criticises them? Abuse has a serious impact on people's upbringing; it can leave serious scars in their lives. But thank God for Jesus who came to die for us, and gave us liberty. Now we can find healing and deliverance from and in Him.

One of my most painful experiences occurred when a man and a woman conspired to put me in trouble, by misusing documents belonging to our ministry. They turned against me when they couldn't get what they wanted. They caused so much trouble, that our organisation was nearly shut down – this was what they wanted.

I was hurting so much, and I went to seek the Lord in prayer, with one of the pastors. As we were praying, God stopped me and dropped a message in my spirit: "Love them; bear the infirmities of the weak". I asked God, "How can I love people who want to destroy my life, and Your ministry?" God insisted that I should love them and He gave me Romans 15:1-3 (New King James Version). It starts with 'We then who are strong ought to bear with the scruples of the weak.' I stopped praying, and told the pastor who was praying with me, of the message that God had given me. She was amazed!

I later called the couple, and told them that I loved them and I forgave them. I believe that because of this, God overturned the situation, and God vindicated me. Since then, I have applied this principle whenever anyone does anything to me. Believe me, it works. If you don't love, you will hate.

Evil will be in your heart, and you will wish evil upon the person that has hurt you.

> *But I say to you, love your enemies, bless those who curse you, do good to those who hate you, and pray for those who spitefully use you and persecute you*
>
> Matthew 5:44

> *Hatred stirs up strife, But love covers all sins*
>
> Proverbs 10:12

## Where is the love?

If we are a society that looks after one another, being kindly affectionate one to another with brotherly love, in honour preferring one another as mentioned in Romans 12:10, the world will be a different   and better place to live in. The world is hurting because there is no love of God in us.  All that the world needs now is genuine love that comes from a pure heart. With the love of God in our hearts, we can change the world. We can look after each other by being in one accord. Let us change this world together, with the love of God.  We only can practice this love, if we have in our hearts the love of God which is in Christ Jesus. God bless you richly as you meditate on these words. Amen.

## PRAYER OF SALVATION

'Dear Jesus I confess that you are my Lord and Personal Saviour. And I believe in my heart that you died and rose again. Father, forgive me of all my sins and cleanse me from all unrighteousness.

Come into my life today and come in to stay. Amen.'